Helping the Wright Brothers

HAPPY READING!

This book is especially for:

_____

Author Suzanne Tate
and
Illustrator James Melvin

Helping the Wright Brothers

A Tale of First Flight Helpers

Suzanne Tate

Illustrated by James Melvin

Nags Head Art
Number 2 of Suzanne Tate's History Series

To Dan Tate
Wright-hand Helper

Library of Congress Catalog Card Number 99-70733
ISBN 978-1-878405-25-8
ISBN 1-878405-25-X
Published by
Nags Head Art, Inc., P.O. Box 2149, Manteo, NC 27954

There is a place in North Carolina that is famous!
Kitty Hawk is its name.

Kitty Hawk

The place is famous because it is the home of First Flight —
where the Wright Brothers first flew their flying machine.

This is a story about members of the Tate family
who lived at Kitty Hawk.
They helped the Wright Brothers
in important ways.

But the tale begins earlier with two Tate brothers
named William and Dan.
In 1850, they left their home in Maine and sailed south.

The Tate brothers wanted to go to Virginia.
But the ship's captain sailed right past there!

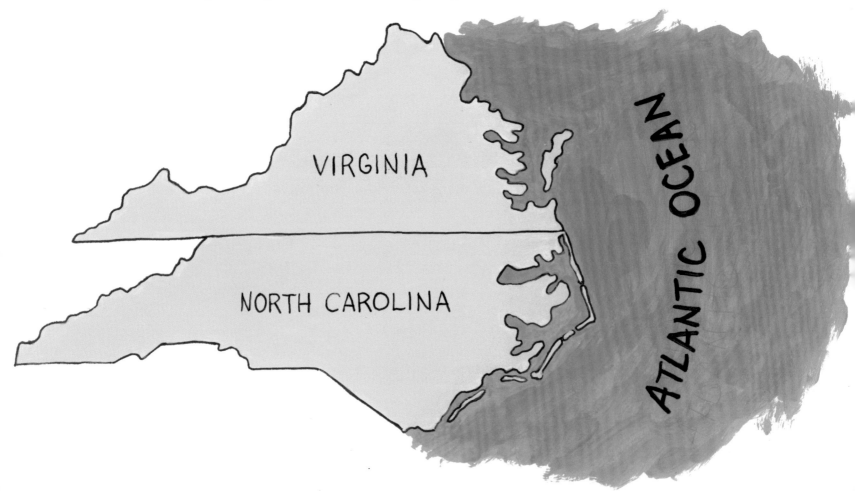

VIRGINIA

NORTH CAROLINA

ATLANTIC OCEAN

When the ship was near North Carolina, William and Dan asked the captain to sail close to shore.

They had a daring plan — they would jump off the ship and swim for land!

William and Dan Tate were brave men
when they jumped overboard.
But they quickly found themselves in trouble!
The tide was stronger than they knew.

Friendly fishermen from Kitty Hawk saw them
and pulled them from the ocean.

The Tate brothers liked North Carolina.
They decided to stay there
and begin new lives.

Dan opened a little grocery store.

William helped start a life-saving station on the beach at Kitty Hawk and was the first keeper there. He remembered how his brother and he were rescued.

William's two sons grew up in the little village.
Their names were Bill and Dan.
Young Dan grew up and made his living by catching
and selling fish.

His brother Bill — quite a bit younger —
would go by his Uncle Dan's store.
"Why aren't you in school?" his uncle asked one day.

"I can only go to the sixth grade here," young Bill replied.
"It costs a lot of money to go away to a school
where I can learn more."

"I'll pay for you to go," his Uncle Dan said.
So young Bill went off to a boarding school
where he lived and studied.

He learned well and came back home.
Later he became a postmaster.

One day, an important letter arrived.
It was from two brothers who lived
in Dayton, Ohio.

The Wright Brothers — Orville and Wilbur —
were asking about Kitty Hawk!

"How often does the wind blow?" they wrote.
"And how tall are your sand hills?"
They needed the right place to test
their glider — a plane without a motor.

They even hoped
one day to . . . FLY!

Bill — the postmaster — was excited.
He wrote to the Wright Brothers right away.
"It's a fine windy place," he told them.
"We have big sand hills — just right
for trying out your glider."

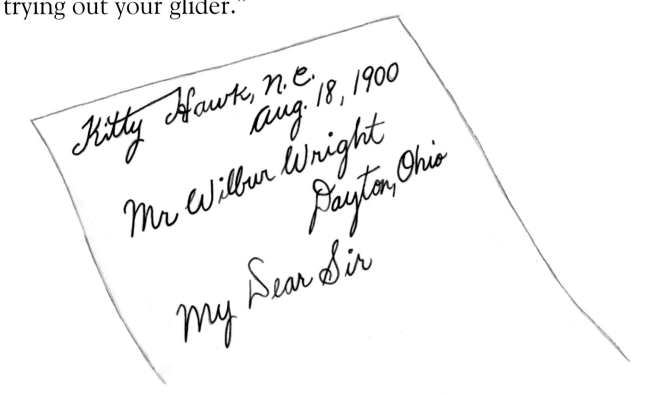

Kitty Hawk, N. C.
aug. 18, 1900
Mr Wilbur Wright
Dayton, Ohio

My Dear Sir

The Wright Brothers were happy to hear
from the young postmaster.
They decided to build a camp at Kitty Hawk.

But first there were many things to do.
They needed a Wright-hand helper!
"I'll tell my brother Dan," Postmaster Bill said.
"He needs extra work when he isn't fishing."

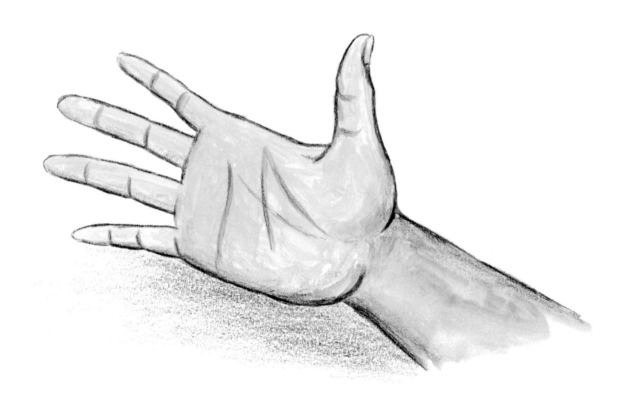

Dan was happy to help the Wright Brothers.
His son, Tommy, liked to help too.
He was a small, lively boy — not afraid to try anything!

When the Wright Brothers were ready to test
their glider, Tommy was ready too.
"I can go up on that," he told them.

"You'll have to ask your father," Orville and Wilbur said.
"Oh, anything I do is all right with him," Tommy boasted.
The Wright Brothers laughed for they often heard him
tell tall tales.

But Papa Dan did agree that Tommy
could ride on the glider.

The young boy climbed onboard
and hung on tight!

The glider went up high above the sand hill.
It bounced and pulled at its lines like a big kite.
Tommy was scared when he looked
at the sand hill below.

The men pulled on the lines
to bring the glider down.

Both Tommy and the glider
came down safely!

That night, he told his little brother Sammy
about his high-flying ride.
Sammy could hardly believe it.

And Tommy's mother said, "I'm sure that's
just another of your tall tales!"

But Papa Dan came in and told them,
"Tommy's tall tale is true this time."
Little Sammy was full of excitement!
"Take me tomorrow too, Papa Dan."

"All right, you can go with us," his father said.
"But you're not big enough to fly!"

Papa Dan and his sons arrived early in the morning
at the Wright Brothers' camp.
The brothers were busy cooking eggs.

They invited the Tates to join them.
Sammy said it was the grandest breakfast
he'd ever had!

After breakfast, the men carried the glider
up the sand hill.

"We will let you ride again today, Tommy,
if that's all right with your papa," Orville said.
"Yes, it helps us in our tests," Wilbur added.

Once more, Tommy climbed onboard the glider.
The wind picked it up, and he was in the air again.

"I'm glad I can help," he thought.

Orville and Wilbur made many other tests with gliders.
One time, Bill's wife loaned them her sewing machine
to sew the cloth for wings.

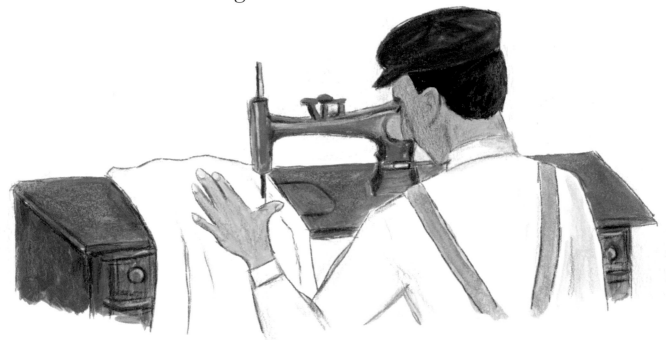

When the testing was done, the Wright Brothers
worked on a motor for a flying machine.

On December 17, 1903, there was big news at Kitty Hawk!
Orville Wright had flown a powered flying machine.
It was the famous First Flight!

Tommy heard about it and ran to tell his father.
Papa Dan was at the country store.

When he heard the news, he jumped up and shouted,
"I knew they could fly, I knew they could fly!
Those Wright Brothers have done it at last."